Dirty Talk

A Guide To Using Nasty Language That Will Make Your Spouse Beg To Spend More Time With You. In Addition, Several Excellent Instances

(How To Learn, With Examples Of Lustful Phrases, To Have A Wonderful Sex Experience With Your Partner, Whether They Are A Man Or A Woman)

Reinhart Danner

TABLE OF CONTENT

Introduction 1

Sexuality Education For Elementary And Middle School Students 11

How To Live Up To A Woman's Expectations . 17

Everyone Is Participating In It. 38

Trust As Well As Communication 42

Absolute Sexual Liberation 58

Establish A Connection On An Affective Level 64

What Is Sexting 68

Why People Enjoy Delving Into Naughty Topics So Much 71

How To Add Humor And Appeal To Your Written Communications 81

The Question Concerning Birds And Bees 90

Guidelines For Unclean Conversations 115

Men's Psychology: A Look Inside The Minds Of Men 126

Restoring The Appeal Of The Attraction 133

Sexuality And Having Children 138

Here Are Four Ways That You Can Make Indecent Talk More Enjoyable. 154

Demand Effort From Her In Exchange For The Information. 158

School Learning 164

Find Out If She Is Interested In You And How To Tell 169

Things That Can Get You And Your Partner Talking About Sexuality To Start A Conversation 176

Introduction

Some guys believe that in order to make a woman horny, they have to whip out their excessively long penises and flaunt it in front of the woman's face. These guys are mistaken. They not only risk seeming extremely silly, but there is also a chance that they may get busted for indecent exposure. The phenomenon in which a woman's sexual desire can be aroused just by having a conversation with her. There are many women who enjoy dirty talk, but you should be careful to only engage in it when the situation is appropriate. If you were to say something to the effect of "I want to squeeze your pink nips," for instance, a female coworker would probably report you for sexual harassment and you would be fired.

If you want to get your girlfriend or wife horny for you, you may (and SHOULD) talk dirty to them. This will make them more interested in having sexual encounters with you. You will discover in this book the killer ways in which you may use dirty talk to make a lady feel both physically and sexually excited.

Words are a potent tool that you may use to turn her on and make her want you more than anything else in the world. Dirty things said to a woman in the appropriate manner will have her drenching herself in desire for you.

At their core, women are creatures of language. What gets them excited is very different from what gets men excited. You can activate them if you are able to paint a picture with only a few carefully chosen words. Therefore, it is in the best interest of men to learn how to say the appropriate dirty things.

Talking trash may be as uncomfortable as walking through a

minefield at times. Because they have never been taught the basic guidelines, many individuals feel completely ashamed and ridiculous at the thought of doing it. This is because they have never been taught the basic guidelines.

When someone says, "Talk dirty to me baby..." in the bedroom, "Talk dirty to me baby..." The hopefully-soon-to-be nasty talker froze up like a roll of dripping wet toilet paper that has been thrown out of an igloo in Antarctica.

"What Am I Supposed to Say? What is it that they want me to answer? Could I take things to an extreme? What if I can't go as far as I want to or if I just come across as lame or stupid?

Dirty conversation is an aspect of eroticism that is sometimes neglected yet possesses a great deal of power. It will activate the magic, supercharge your sexual polarity, and add a steamy layer of liberty to your nude shenanigans.

Dirty conversation, much like dirty clothes, is something that has to be calibrated to whoever is receiving it. much like dirty clothes, dirty talk needs to be calibrated. Maybe something that you consider to be "dirty talk" is something that the other person does not find offensive, silly, or just plain nuts, and vice versa.

How exactly does one go about talking dirty to a woman? This may be difficult for many men, but knowing how to talk dirty to her does not require you to be a genius, nor does it demand you to be a god of exes. All you need is little practice. You simply have to have an understanding of your woman and the needs she has. Talking dirty is often not a topic that guys want to discuss with their friends, which is one of the reasons why it is so simple to experience feelings of isolation and confusion. Thankfully, this book and others like it are dedicated to teaching men how to talk dirty to woman. Other books in this genre also cover the same ground. Your lady will think she is really fortunate after you have mastered the situation and are able to relax in it thanks to your efforts.

Read on if you need some basic tips and ideas to learn how to talk dirty to a woman and deliver hot and irresistible dirty talk. If you want to learn how to talk dirty to a woman, you should keep reading. Before we get started, there is one thing you need to be aware of, and that is the fact that you need to have an open mind, and there is a good chance that you will need to push yourself beyond of your comfort zone.

If you are reading this, there is a good chance that you are at a loss for words when it comes to communicating with the woman you are dating, your girlfriend, or your wife. Dirty talk is something that women like just as much as men do, and in some cases even more. There is no question about this. The fact that mental magic and telepathy may have just as much of an effect as actual physical touch.

When it comes to learning how to talk dirty to a woman, the most important thing you can do is build up your confidence. Confidence does not mean acting like a big shot or letting your ego fly; rather, it simply means delivering what you say to your woman with confidence. Confidence does not mean acting like a big shot and letting your ego fly. If you are concerned about making a fool of yourself when you first begin, then you should know that there is a good chance that this may really occur.

Men and women are two very different kinds of creatures. You are making the BIGGEST mistake possible if you believe that your woman wants to hear what you would "love" to hear about yourself. Although there is certainly some overlap in terms of what men and women love to hear, the fact that women have different buttons that need to be pushed is an important consideration.

Women adore the feeling of being desired and required, as well as being the only person in the world who can fulfill their needs. The very last thing you want to do is quote lines from adult movies since doing so may earn you a dirty look or a confused expression such as "what the hell did you just say?"

Start out with some naughty text messages that will get rid of the tension, give you the opportunity to test the water, and let you see how your woman reacts. A quick and simple way to get her excited would be to send her a text message. and have her spend the week kneeling at your feet, especially if the two of you are apart from one another and preoccupied with your respective jobs.

The word "anticipation" is a major turn on. Talk to her about all the naughty things you want to do to her over the phone or send her a message via text. The most important thing is to make it about her and just about her! If you can make her feel desired, needed, and sexually attractive, you will be amazed at how easily you can turn up the heat in the bedroom.

You may engage in dirty talk when you are out in public by either whispering something that you want to do to her when you get back home OR telling her that you want to take her right then and there. Do not mumble or fumble your way through your dirty talk, regardless of the strategy you choose to employ. Be positive and self-assured, and establish yourself as THE man.

When you are face to face with one another, you will be able to tell her how sizzling he is and how much he gets you turned on. Women have egos just like men do, so you need to make sure you push the right buttons and give her the impression that she is the only one for you and the only one you want. Whisper in her ear all of the things that you are aware that she loves it when you do to her, as well as the inappropriate things that she loves to do to you.

It is essential to go with your gut instinct and pay attention to how he reacts. Making eye contact with her and giving her "that look" might cause her to lose her balance and wobble on her knees. It will astound you how effective eye contact and an authoritative voice, look, and approach can be in convincing her to beg for more of what you have to offer.

It is important to tone it up and down depending on where you are in the world. When you are out with your friends or going out to dinner, you have the opportunity to behave inappropriately. Like As I've noted in the past, hostility may make a woman want to rip your clothing off as soon as the two of you are left alone together. The ability to know when to raise the stakes is one that can only be gained through experience. You need to be careful and act appropriately, you can't just rush in there and expect to make her excited. There are some women who enjoy very "hard" dirty talk, just like there are some men who enjoy it.

Sexuality Education For Elementary And Middle School Students

The child is seven years old at the present time. The young man's lifelong ambition to attend school was finally realized when he registered for classes. There were now a lot of new friends and allies. At this point in time, the child's primary focus is on school-related activities. This is the reason why, in comparison to preschool and adolescence, this period appears to be one of relative peace for parents.

In the body of a child who is in junior school, a complicated reorganization of the work of the body's most essential functional systems takes place. Additionally, the child's brain undergoes rapid growth, reaching 1 kilogram (whereas in a newborn, it weighs 350 grams). As a result of the activation of the second signaling system, the cerebral hemispheres, and in particular the frontal lobes, grow in a very distinctive manner. Alterations also take place in the course of the excitation and inhibition of the fundamental neurological processes, and the probability of inhibitory reactions grows as a result. This is a physiological prerequisite for the formation of several volitional qualities in the child, and it increases the child's ability to demonstrate independence, control impulsive actions, and consciously restrain unwanted actions. This is particularly important when it comes to the formation of friendly relationships between boys and girls.

When there is more harmony between the child's nervous system processes, it is easier for the child to restructure his behavior in accordance with the expectations of adults.

- "The junior school years are a time for assimilating new information and building your knowledge base... The characteristics of children at this age, which include trusting obedience to authority, enhanced receptivity, alertness, and a naive playful attitude toward many of the things they experience, are favorable to the proper performance of this vital function. 1. When it comes to sexual education for younger pupils, parents should base their approach on these psychological features of their children.

During the years spent in school, gender variations in the physiological systems of the body of boys and girls start to become more easily discernible. For instance, by the age of seven, boys already have a higher chest circumference than girls do. When compared to boys, girls experience a minor delay in development and weight gain beginning around the age of nine or ten. The female body is generally considered to be more frail than the male body. Overworked and mentally and physically exhausted girls are more likely to be of the female gender. Therefore, when it comes to education, one ought to take into account both age and gender.

In addition to the physiological variations between the sexes, there are also discernible disparities in the psychological features of boys and girls, most notably in the way that their interests are structured. Boys are more interested in their device's internal construction, whereas girls are more interested in the overall features and purposes of the objects they examine. Because of this, guys are more prone to take items apart, such as watches or toys, in order to investigate what is contained within them and analyze the mechanisms that make them function.

Children of this age are beginning to develop a greater awareness of their gender. They exhibit behavior connected to the reawakening of sexual drives, which is a defining trait of this group. The guys appear to be interested in anything and everything that has to do with the dynamic between males and females. Children, and particularly young girls, are obsessed with their appearance. Boys grow into masculine characteristics, including a desire to aid and protect girls. However, there are cases in which a young lady will scale a fence, engage in war games, or play chase while carrying a toy machine gun or a sword. In this situation, she needs to be reminded that she is a girl and should not act like a boy; conversely, if the boy is distressed and sobbing, he is informed that he is whimpering like a girl and that he should stop acting like a girl.

The perspectives that boys and girls hold towards the many topics covered in school are distinct from one another. For instance, girls are better at calculating arithmetic operations in mathematics lessons, although it is not difficult for boys to establish arithmetic causality. This difference can be attributed to gender differences in learning styles. In terms of academic performance, there is a gender gap: more females have high academic achievement and are exceptional students.

How To Live Up To A Woman's Expectations

The majority of people will tell you to ignore their advice and simply be yourself. This is incredibly useful and sound advice, and it is also advice that you should follow even if you are lazy. This piece of advice has repeatedly shown to be an effective strategy for ensuring that one will wind up with a broken heart. Consider for a moment that you are about to compete in a boxing battle on the ring; will you walk in there and simply express yourself by punching your opponent in any way that comes to mind, regardless of who they are? No, of course not, unless you want to look like a crazy person who has their face buried in the carpet. Keep in mind that this is a never-ending war that the majority of guys consistently lose. Do not be like them, and especially do not continue to be like them. However, if you feel that you are already masculine enough and that she will truly adore you for who you truly are, then you should go ahead and be yourself.

The Unknown Facts

You aren't truly interested in just living up to her expectation. You have to go beyond that. The only way to win is to engage in sexual communication since doing so will enable you to enter the ring while holding a spear in one hand. Because she is not accustomed to this mode of conflict, she experiences anxiety whenever she thinks about engaging in it. During the same time, this will spark her wildest imaginations. You will be able to influence her imaginations as well as into her mind if you do this.

It's all about how you feel.

What exactly is it that we feel? An emotion is "a conscious mental reaction (such as anger or fear) subjectively experienced as strong feeling usually directed toward a specific object and typically accompanied by changes in the body's physiology and behavior," as stated in the Merriam-Webster Dictionary.

As you can see, a person's emotions can bring about changes in both their physiological and behavioral states. For instance, if you insult your professor in front of the class, he will feel bad and may even give you a low grade, or even worse, a failing grade. This is because he will be embarrassed for himself. You may expect that the link of friendship between the two of you will strengthen, and that she will even trust you more, if you are there for a friend whenever she is experiencing difficulty and you soothe her during the ordeal.

The expression of one's feelings is essential to effective sexual communication.

Using Emotions to Manipulate Others

Emotions are invisible energies that are responsible for producing changes in reality. These energies are the driving force behind our experiences. Once you have mastered the art of manipulating emotions, you will be able to control how a woman responds to you. This is tied to how you want her to think and feel about you when she considers her relationship with you.

It is essential to keep in mind that women are not exempt from blame in relation to this issue. REASON FOR: They are also masters of the art of manipulation. There are a lot of women who toy with guys as if they were puppets with strings tied to their bodies, so that the men have no option but to respond in the way that the women want. Avoid having this occur to you at all costs.

Love within Boundaries: A Guide to Creating Comfortable Distances Between You and Your Partner

Do you hover over your daughter to the point where she becomes overwhelmed with worry, and then you wonder why she becomes irritable.

That is typically how we behave.

Let's examine how this operates in the context of your marriage or your connection with your partner. Lie down next to him with your face pressed up against his and your bodies pressed together in a close embrace.

How much longer are you going to lie like that? After sitting inside for a bit, you'll feel the urge to go outside and take in some oxygen-rich air. Do you find yourself embarrassed as a result of that feeling?

This is something that mothers frequently do to their daughters, essentially "breathing in their faces" and never letting them catch their breath. We behave in the same way in all of our interactions, which results in the creation of unhealthy distances.

Everyone requires a certain amount of personal space. Some demand an extremely large circle, while others require only a small amount of breathing room. Even if you haven't realized it yet, you require some personal space in order to function properly.

Any intrusion into someone's personal space, no matter how slight, can be considered harmful. One person's integrity can be severely damaged by a single insult, a single phrase, or even a tiny humiliation. Because of this, it is essential to have a conversation with your daughter about the need of respecting personal boundaries. Without them, it is hard to have meaningful relationships that are healthy.

If she is having trouble determining what constitutes a personal boundary or the required distance between herself and other people, then she should ask herself the following questions for assistance:

"Is this a question I can answer without hesitation? Is there an absence of tact in it?

"Am I prepared to bear this suffering and melancholy that is being heaped upon me?"

"Was it you who suggested that I do this?"

"Is this a criticism that I am prepared to take on board? From where does it originate?

"Is it absolutely vital that I carry out the tasks that have been assigned to me?"

"Am I acting out of guilt or shame by performing this act for the benefit of another person?"

"Am I to give up my own worldview, goals, and aspirations in exchange for those of another person?"

"Am I coming under pressure because of the viewpoints and attitudes I hold?"

"In exchange for me doing something that makes me uncomfortable, am I going to get a promise of love?"

Because I am not speaking up, am I giving another person permission to do as they please? Is there a tacit understanding here?"

"Do I unconsciously help other people break my boundaries?" "Do I help other people break my boundaries?"

"Have I allowed a window or door to remain open to my soul?"

The considerations that should be made in light of the responses to the questions presented above should center on the people that we invite into our private sphere.

Why do we act in such a manner? There are straightforward as well as not so straightforward causes for this practice, which is comprised of a series of actions that all share one thing in common: an inability to establish a healthy space between ourselves and the others.

We are unable to decline offers, and we do not pay attention to what our hearts want. The main components that go into the recipe are doing one's best to help others, being careful not to make any mistakes, and working hard to reach absolute excellence. By restraining our feelings, we are able to keep other people from becoming unhappy. We are willing to put ourselves through any kind of ordeal in order to obtain the results we seek. We violate both our bodies and our souls in the pursuit of monetary gain, respect, recognition, or love. Because we are so preoccupied with the negative, we fail to recognize the positive aspects of our lives and overlook the many things for which we should express gratitude.

Our lives are filled with countless tiny and large personal betrayals that we accept as normal. By betraying ourselves, we are only helping the intruders do damage to our honor and reputation. When careless people go by us, we become like a fragile vase that has been put at the end of a table and shatters into a million pieces as they pass by it.

In point of fact, we have consented to the occurrence of that event. Is the person who was just walking by to blame for the damage? Actually, this wasn't the case; the individual was merely going about his or her normal activities when the edge of the vase got in the way.

The vase in a figurative sense ought to be our most prized possession. We do not secure it by placing it in a safe drawer or a huge closet; rather, we keep it out in the open where anyone can see it. After that, the next step is to give careful consideration to who holds the key to the door; nobody should be allowed in. We allow others to cross our boundaries, and then we sit back and watch as they wreak havoc on our lives while we grin and pretend like nothing is wrong. We regard our very selves, symbolized by the vase, as worthless relics that can be sold at a yard sale for a pittance.

How exactly can your daughter make a difference in all of this? First, by beginning to focus on the relationship that she has with herself, which includes living a life free of coercion and authoritarianism, as well as supporting and believing in herself even when no one else does. A daughter who is able to take care of both her body and her spirit is one who has learned how to establish firm boundaries. She only shares information when she deems it necessary, she pays attention to what she has to say to herself, and she keeps her supplies stocked up.

If she is in a relationship that is causing her pain, you should encourage her to take a step back and keep a safe space between the two of you. She will have a much easier time getting past the painful experience and the negative feelings if she avoids thinking about the issue. When she so chooses, she may make the distance shorter and bring the two of them closer together. This is the most reliable formula for the fulfillment of any loving relationship's potential.

By the way, have you tried your hand at this already? Don't be afraid to try it, and make sure you give yourself permission to do so!

Consider the situation from the viewpoint of the other person at the same time: how frequently do you compromise someone's honor in an effort to become too close to them? Is this potentially the root of all of your disagreements and disagreements with others?

The method: There is no A+B=C formula for successful foreplay; however, the secret is hidden within the word itself. The foreplay itself is the methodology.

Interjection that serves as a warning or condition indicating that something is going to take place. (i.e., in the game of golf, yelling "Fore!" alerts the other golfers that you are about to hit the ball in the direction of them, so they should cover their damn heads!)

To "play" anything means to participate in or engage in an activity that is pleasurable or enjoyable.

Only when you forget that foreplay is supposed to be enjoyable will it lose its sparkle and turn into a tedious activity. There is absolutely NO room for agenda-driven, results-only thinking in excellent foreplay, and there is absolutely NO room for agenda-driven, results-only thinking in good sex.

It is interesting to note that women frequently have their first and sometimes only orgasms during the course of foreplay. This could be one of the reasons why, culturally (at least in American culture in the United States), it has come to be viewed as a 'chore' or even as 'unnecessary' by certain, I'll be generous and call them, people.

Selfishness has no place in healthy sexual relationships.

As we have stated previously, "quickies" are not ideal for a number of reasons, the primary one being that it takes a certain level of skill of the art of excellent sex to give a woman an orgasm in a short amount of time. However, as a general rule, you should give the experience the time it deserves. There are going to be some people who have different opinions on this, and the amount of time and stimulation required will also vary from person to person and over the course of your life.

The following are the overarching instructions:

Once foreplay has begun in earnest, you should resist the urge to rush it, relax, and PLAY. Keep in mind that foreplay is a game of "call and response," and be ready to answer your partner's call. Alter your tempo, position, amount of talking or not talking, music, and other factors until the passion builds to such a point that you and your partner are pleading for it to happen already.

This is the "secret" to having enjoyable pre-play. Calm down. Have fun!

Talk It Over With Your Spouse.

Always check with your spouse to make sure that the two of you are interested in trying this out before you get started with it. Keep in mind that it takes two people to dance the tango, and this rule applies even more so to tantric sex. If you and your partner are interested in carrying it out, you need to be sure that you are both operating from the same playbook. The vast majority of people are unaware of the fact that your partner might not be ready for something like this.

Tantric sex is a two-part process and something that the two of you will have to complete together. Because of this, you will need to discuss this with one another before beginning the process, even though you believe starting right away is a fantastic idea. It is not going to happen if neither of you is interested in cooperating with the other.

In addition, if you are practicing tantric sex but they are not, it would mean that just one of you is going to experience intense orgasms and want to take it slower, while the other will be doing the reverse. If they are practicing tantric sex, however, both of you would benefit from the experience. Do you not think that this is a tad bit unfair? If you try to enjoy tantric sex in any other way, the primary challenge you face is that you won't be able to make it work, and as a result, you won't really achieve the results that you're looking for.

In addition, it shouldn't be too difficult to persuade your partner to give it a shot. After all, you want to have deeper levels of closeness with the other person, as well as better sexual experiences, more levels of desire, and overall more pleasure together.

It shouldn't be hard to win over your partner to this idea given that it's likely something they'll love simply due to the fact that it will spice things up and provide diversity.

Body Preparation Since it takes some time, one of the best things to do before engaging in tantric sex is to get the body ready for it. People frequently have the misconception that tantra evenings are not as physically taxing as they actually are. In many cases, it also helps you have a more positive perception of oneself. You're going to like the way your body feels and the overall sense of wellness that you get from it.

When you are physically in good shape and the room is set up in the appropriate manner, it will calm you down, which will make making love one of the most pleasurable experiences possible.

So, what are some options that are available to you? First things first, if you're not the type of person who wants to put in a lot of time at the gym or put in a lot of effort to improve their physical fitness, you should consider doing yoga.

You're going to find that participating in yoga is one of the best decisions you could make. It is a wonderful item that will assist you in making the most out of your experience.

In addition to this, yoga improves flexibility, and some poses can even bring about positive changes in a person's sexual life. Some of them can even be utilized in the context of tantric sexual practices. In addition to that, it assists in re-aligning the energy.

It has been determined that the energy you possess flow through your spine; hence, you should always ensure that your back is relaxed and that you are not slumped over. You need to ensure that you are not injuring yourself in the process, and that the movement does not have a negative effect on the back in any manner.

Everyone Is Participating In It.

When you take a glance at the world around you and pay attention to what is being discussed by other people, especially among your contemporaries, you can be tempted to hastily draw the conclusion that "Everyone's into this thing; what's the big deal anyway? Why should I be the only one who does this? But let me tell you, doing so would be a complete and utter mistake. It would appear that sexual perversion and superfluity are the things to do these days. Indeed, it may be found everywhere. Without a shadow of a doubt, it appears to be the latest trend. Despite the fact that this is true, one cannot legitimately draw the conclusion that everyone is engaging in inappropriate sexual behavior. I can tell you without a shadow of a doubt that what you've heard is not accurate.

There are a number of persons your age, both male and female, and maybe even right there where you are, who are intent on carrying out activities in the appropriate manner (God's manner). It's possible that you haven't heard of them because such people rarely flaunt their accomplishments. They aren't like those "empty barrels" who make a lot of noise; rather, they appreciate the elegance that comes from chastity draped in humility. Because of this, they do not want to boast about the unusual way they live their lives. Some children, both male and female, are not prepared to deal with the teasing that may come their way if their friends find out. One of the primary reasons that some young women want to conceal the fact that they are virgins is the worry that they may be the victim of sexual assault. Therefore, everything boils down to the perspective that one chooses to take and the things that one decides to put their faith in.

Permit me to ask you this question: would you rather fit in with the throng that is making mistakes, or would you rather stand out for doing what is right? It is completely clear to me that going along with the herd is a terribly wasteful strategy. However, I would like it to be brought to your attention that it is also the most cost-effective method of achieving insignificance. To win the crown, you will almost always need to distinguish yourself from the other competitors. Walking the route of the few could make one feel as though they are swimming against the current, but the reality is that there is honor and glory at the end of that journey. You get to decide which option to go with! It is not too late to take a stance that can make a difference. You can return to God and begin again, even if at some point you fell short of what was expected of you.

Trust As Well As Communication

Here is an ideal method for discussing ANY issue that you are facing, and it will only set you back a few dollars. I need you to go out and purchase TWO sleep masks, which are those things that cover your eyes to prevent light from entering so that you can sleep during the day.

After we have had some time to calm down after our massive argument, I want the two of you to put on the sleep masks. You are free to discuss the issue at hand now. Does it really sound that easy?

When you both put on your sleep masks, neither of you will be able to observe the other person's facial expressions.

This will assist you in focusing on genuinely talking it out with the other person. It's similar to texting, but you won't get calluses on your thumbs.

I'd like for one of you to start talking while the other one listens to what you have to say. To truly listen to the other person without responding will require some self-control throughout this stage of the conversation. When one side withdraws their protest, the other side will react.

You shouldn't go on to another problem unless you've figured out how to put an end to the current one first.

In a society where everything needs to be done quickly, you should try to take a step back and look at whatever it is that has angered you from both sides. When there is a problem, our natural inclination is to overreact to it.

If you want your relationship to be successful in the long run, you need to locate a middle ground and talk about any issues in a level-headed manner until a solution is found. There are to be no secrets!

Take it or leave it, but always remember to stick up for yourself, that is the piece of advise I have for you, young man.

The Third Chapter

1. Exert your independence.

The allure of a good surprise is not to be underestimated. You and your lover should take a shower together, you should get some new lingerie and wear it, and you should surprise your partner with a deep, passionate kiss when they are expecting you to merely touch their lips.

2. Practice good health.

Eating healthily and engaging in regular exercise help you get in better touch with your body. This inner healthy glow not only helps you seem more appealing, but it also bestows an abundance of energy upon you and makes you experience a heightened sense of vitality and aliveness.

3. Show your partner some love.

If you haven't had sexual activity in a while, it's probably best to work your way back into the swing of things by taking things slowly at first. Instead of attempting to go from a standing start to racing speed, ease back into the physical by touching when you can and by being respectful with each other. attempting to get from a standing start to racing speed is like trying to go from a standing start to driving at full speed. When you talk, touch each other. When you walk past each other in the corridor, stop and give each other a kiss. While they are seated and reading a magazine, run your finger up the top of their shoulder. Make yourself comfortable on the couch while watching your go-to movie.

4. Exude sexual allure.

When your significant other gets home from a long day, surprise them with a foot soak that contains peppermint. Massage their hands, scalp, back, or wherever else that strikes your fancy (if you don't know how to massage, don't think about it; just do what feels good and go with the flow). You could even go for a more delicate feel by draping your lover in silk scarves or feathers and running them around their body.

5. When your partner accomplishes something you appreciate, be supportive to them.

Even if the two of you have been together for a very long time, your significant other might not always know what it is that you enjoy doing, and even if they do, it doesn't hurt to let them know every once in a while.

Say what you like and why you like it; you never know what someone who knows more about you can come up with to make you happy if they have more information.

6. Before turning in for the night, read your lover a titillating narrative.

Any effort to bring your sexual life back from the dead must first focus on the mind. It is necessary to turn it on first, and after that is done, the body will follow. You can try Nancy Friday if you want to read about other people's sexual dreams, or you can read some of the fantastic erotic fiction that is currently available.

7. Have a good time

When was the last time the three of you shared a good laugh? Play your favorite song while you get down on the dance floor. You could even purchase music that was popular during the time when the three of you first met and play that while you eat supper together to take a trip down memory lane. Participate in an evening swim.

8. Compose a sexually suggestive letter

Writing it down is a terrific option to telling your spouse what you want them to do to you in case you are unable to communicate this verbally. It enables you to be as detailed as you want without the fear that your face is going to turn the color of a tomato, and it provides your partner with the opportunity to analyze what you've said and get into the mood after you've done so.

9. Try new things

Acquire a brand new skill side by side. Consider taking a weekend trip somewhere romantic. You might also experiment with a sex toy, choosing one from the many that are available. If you always have sex while lying down, you should consider having sex while standing or sitting instead. If you are consistently in first place, you should consider rearranging the deck.

10. Bring your attention to the present moment.

When you get down to business, it is absolutely necessary for you to keep your attention fixed on the activity at hand. To accomplish this, you need to silence the constant chattering in your thoughts.

It is not important that you forgot to pick up the dry cleaning, that you need to phone your mother to wish her a happy birthday, or that you have run out of cereal. You shouldn't worry about these things. Put all of those material aside for a later time. After a long time. After you've finished, it probably won't seem nearly as significant to you anymore.

For Maggie

In that split second before the unmistakable roar fills the space, I feel a tightening in my stomach. The aftereffects of the Pop-Tart snack that we consumed in the wee hours of the morning have passed.

James makes a snide remark, saying that "Our Angel isn't immortal... she needs food."

The boys slowly pull themselves away from me despite their reluctance. I have no doubt that they are starving as well.

After locating my glasses and making my way to the kitchen on unsteady knees, I take a quick look at the time displayed on the microwave and then at the road outside the window. "Oh my God, guys. We have to be at Mom and Dad's in two hours, and the drive there will take us half an hour in this snow, and we absolutely have to take a shower before we leave."

I take the wrapper off of another Pop-Tart pack and remove one of the pastries from the package. It is Ford who consumes the second pastry. Before devouring the delicious, frosted, chocolate-filled center, I nibble on the perimeter of the pastry, skipping the step of toasting it first.

Even if they don't understand what the big deal is, my brothers always follow in my footsteps. It's almost as if they're puppy love gone bad since they won't allow me get more than a foot away from them. The fact that I am so cherished by them gives me confidence and elevates my sense of uniqueness, which is the exact opposite of how I viewed myself before yesterday night. My stride is more buoyant and my view is more optimistic as a direct result of the many things I've discovered about myself over the years.

If not because of the fact that we are stepsiblings, but at least because of the abnormal nature of our relationship, our parents might get upset if they find out that we are getting together.

After drinking all of the water that was left in the cup of someone else that was sitting on the counter, I make my way to the restroom. The boys are closing in quickly on me. I had never given much consideration to how good my behind looked, but after hearing all of their praise, I have no problem with them following me about.

I turn back just in time to see Ford grabbing my toothbrush as I adjust the temperature of the shower water.

"Whoa! Put that in writing.

"Why? What's the matter?" He examines the toothbrush by holding it up to the light. "Do you use this to clean your fishbowl or something?" "Is this what you use to clean it?"

"No, that's what I use to clean the plaque off my teeth."

"You made a wise choice in selecting a toothbrush. The dorky spectacles that you're wearing aren't only for looks." Ford has a good laugh at his own jokes. "I had every intention of brushing my teeth."

"You can't make use of my toothbrush."

Although Heath and James are currently leaning against the counter and watching, it is difficult for me to determine how they feel about using a communal toothbrush. Nobody comes to my defense when I need them. It's possible that they take pleasure in watching their brother be denied, and that's all it is.

"Why on earth not?" Ford inquires.

"That's a nasty thing."

"Do you need me to point out where you've been talking with your mouth? Or that you drank out of my water cup only a moment ago?"

I give him the middle finger and shake it.

He just stands there looking at me in complete quiet. I quickly grab the toothbrush out of his hand as the steam from the shower begins to escape, capitalizing on the split second that it takes for him to turn his focus to the steam.

"Alright, I guess I'll just have to use my finger." Ford opens the top drawer, grabs the tube of toothpaste, and unscrews the cap on the tube of toothpaste.

As his fingers begin to wrap around the malleable container, my anxiety levels begin to grow. Oh no! He is an expert at crushing tubes. When we were children, this drove me absolutely bonkers.

"Wait!" I attempt to get the toothpaste out of the cabinet, but it's already too late. The evidence that the damage has been done can be seen on his finger in the form of an excessively lengthy strip of paste.

Everyone looks at me as I throw both my hands up in the air and let out a sigh of exasperation.

You don't share toothpaste with anyone else, do you? Heath inquires, displaying a high level of bewilderment.

I clench my teeth and pounce on Ford's hand as he's holding the tube. I had forgotten that you were such a tube crusher. Take a look at this!

They are still staring, but one or both of their expressions is beginning to alter to one of surprise or disbelief.

I prop the scrambled container up with my hand. "You really screwed things up this time."

"What does it even matter?"

"I roll my eyes and murmur, "There is no way that this will ever work."

"That's exactly what you said right before I proved that my cock could, in fact, fit inside of you," I said. Ford manages to keep the tone light.

I can only nod my head. "Does the sense of humor of men ever evolve?"

James elucidates, "Not really," the statement.

I manage to get Heath's attention, but all he does is smirk and shrug. "It made me laugh."

Ford manages to settle his nerves. "Okay, but let's be serious: why does it make a difference if we compress it from the top or the middle?"

The instruction was to "squeeze from the bottom." Heath gives a chuckle while prodding Ford with his elbow and smiling.

Absolute Sexual Liberation

The tale of Leslie:

At the age of fourteen, I began to experience a great deal of perplexity, loneliness, and a significant absence in my life. I was subjected to a great deal of temptation, and as a result, I started going out more, hanging out with males, and eventually, I started having sexual encounters. It seemed like every one of my friends was doing it. I desired to understand and participate in the activities and sensations that they were having. After that, I was taken aback because it did not have the same sensation that I had anticipated it to have.

I had the impression that I was being taken advantage of, and as a result, I started using drugs and drinking alcohol.

However, neither of those things helped me feel any better. In point of fact, they made my condition even more dire. This was my life for the past five years, and neither of my parents had any idea what was going on.

It was unbelievable that I hadn't become pregnant yet, and there came a day when I was certain that the test would come back positive. At the pregnancy clinic, I was alone myself in the counseling room the entire time. Nobody, not even my partner, was aware that I had been there. If I were pregnant, I would have preferred to find out the news on my own.

My room was visited by the nurse, who informed me that the results of the pregnancy test came back negative. After she had left, the counselor began asking me questions that I had never been asked by anybody else before. She was extremely nice to me, but she didn't beat about the bush when she told me how fortunate it was that I wasn't pregnant. She inquired about my contingency plans in the event that I became pregnant. She inquired about the boy I was dating, wanting to know if he was someone I could put my faith in to take care of me. She inquired as to whether or not I was aware of the fact that the fact that I had made the decision to engage in sexual activity in the past did not compel me to engage in sexual activity in the present or in the future. She expressed it in a way that I had not really given much thought to before. I had a decision to make! I was still in charge of the direction that my life would take.

She walked me through the process of starting anew in a step-by-step manner. After that, I was unable to have sexual encounters. It was not simple, and the only reason it was successful was because I met with the lady at the clinic on a weekly basis, and she ensured that I was accountable for my actions. She shared with me how precious I am to others as well as the incredibly bright future that lay in wait for me.

Don't get the wrong impression. I continued to be tempted, and there were moments when I surrounded myself with the wrong people and put myself in situations where I was vulnerable. However, I realized that I needed to shake up my routine and get rid of the situations that were too tempting. As for me, I ended things with my boyfriend. I had no idea how challenging this would be; in reality, it was more simpler than I had anticipated. When I informed him I thought I might be pregnant, he inquired as to whether or not it would be his child. That shattered my world. After that, I told him that I no longer wanted to have sex with him, at which point he became angry and called me stupid. He went so far as to say that the woman who worked at the clinic was some kind of religious nut job who was obviously controlling me. The way he responded made it abundantly clear that I needed to move on.

I had to hear the message multiple times before I was finally able to wrap my head around the idea that my sexuality is a gift that I am able to exercise control over. A year later, when I first entered college, I was still immersed in the sexual subculture of the campus. But I started to become aware of how much emotional suffering was connected to the fact that my friends were having sexual encounters. I had a friend who became pregnant but ultimately decided to terminate the pregnancy. I also had a friend who got intoxicated and couldn't remember who she had sex with. The anecdotes never failed to make me grateful for the choice I had taken to go in a different direction.

The conviction that I have in my heart to abstain from sexual activity until the night of my wedding is sincere, but it hasn't been easy to maintain. I want to be with someone who loves and respects me, who will support me and listen to what I have to say, and who wants the best for me. I want someone who pursues me in a healthy way and who loves me for who I am, not for what I do or don't do.

Establish A Connection On An Affective Level

It is essential to be able to connect with any woman if one want to be able to know how to attract any given female. That is, how to forge an emotional connection with her in such a way that she feels physically close to you and you feel physically close to her.

Utilizing the "I" viewpoint while having a conversation is one strategy that may be utilized to cultivate an emotional connection with a girl. Direct communication of your viewpoints, beliefs, and, most importantly, feelings is encouraged.

Create an atmosphere of sexual tension via the use of touch.

There is no such thing as an adequate article on how to attract women that does not include at least one suggestion on how to create sexual tension and directly want sexual activity.

After all, this is what prevents you from being added to the friend list.

Touching a woman physically is one of the most powerful ways to build sexual tension with her. Touching each other early on in your conversation by lightly tapping the back of your hand on her elbow is an easy way to start.

If she is comfortable with that touch, you might gradually increase the amount of physical contact you have with her for longer periods of time in more personal areas (shoulder, back, thigh, face). If she is comfortable with that touch, you could gradually increase the amount of physical contact you have with her.

When do you touch more (or less) (or less) when do you touch more (or less)

Checking for compliance is the most important step to do if you want to know whether you should touch more or less. If she lets you touch her or starts touching you back, then you have permission to take things a step further with your touch.

If, on the other hand, she flinches or moves away when you touch her, you should give her some space. Create a more relaxed atmosphere by joking about and establishing an emotional connection with the other person. When she is more at ease, you should make another attempt to heighten the sexual tension through physical contact.

A man who places a high value on himself is not afraid to pursue a woman to whom he is attracted, but while he is doing so, he treats her with the utmost respect.

What Is Sexting

The term "sexting" refers to a combination of sexual activity with electronic messaging. The practice of sending sexually explicit instant messages is referred to as "sexting." Sending bare or seminude photographs of yourself, as well as recordings of yourself speaking clearly, is sometimes an additional need.

Sexting can take place through the use of text messaging on mobile devices or through other messaging services, as well as through direct messaging through web-based media locales.

Sexting Is Permitted At This Gathering, Which Includes People of All Ages. Whatever the Case May Be, Well-This kind of sexual association is likely going to be utilized by well-informed adolescents and younger adults.

focuseson the evidence that almost one in six children and one in four adolescents have engaged in the practice of sending or receiving a sexually explicit text message (sext). Sexting is something that interests three out of every four young adults still in their teen years.

At its most fundamental level, sexting consists of two individuals voluntarily messaging one another about their sexual fantasies. It is typically as simple as quickly recalling a memory (e.g., "The Evening Before Was So Warm, I Cherished the Manner in Which You Pushed Me in a Tough Spot"), or it may be a 10-section sensual novel that your companion composes specifically for you by means of message with almost no expectation for a reaction other than "thank you." In either case, it is likely to be as simple as quickly recalling a memory. Sexting can involve sending written messages, as well as pictures, videos, or even voice messages in addition to those sent electronically.

Sexting, like many types of telephone sexual encounters, is an amazing way to connect with your partner from a long distance, build sexual tension in the middle of rendezvous, or even investigate dreams, all of which are activities in which you might not feel comfortable engaging in while you are actually in the same room with them.

Why People Enjoy Delving Into Naughty Topics So Much

Some people delight in filthy conversation because they have a robust and lively mental picture bank to draw on. When people hear a description that is both alluring and nasty, they are able to conjure up an image that not only actualizes the experience but also adds to the excitement and eroticism of the encounter. These people often have an open mind and do not pass judgment on others. Having a good session of filthy discussion suggests that you and your partner are comfortable with each other, which can only improve your sex life regardless of what it is that you are doing physically. However, even without penetration, some women (and some men) might get so turned on by obscene chat that they orgasm without any genital stimulation at all, or they only demand a little bit more. This can happen even when there is no physical contact between the partners. convey feelings of pleasure throughout their bodies. Yes, engaging in sleazy discussion packs quite a punch, and we can see why some of us look forward to it. Is it not the case that the brain is among the body's most significant sexual organs? Even when the erogenous zones of our bodies fail to react to sexy settings, our minds may dream up hot scenarios to get us in the mood for some naughty behavior. And sexual conversations don't have to take place at the same time as the act itself. "Having a sexual chat with your partner before engaging in sexual activity might pique their interest and put them in an excited state as a result of your tease. A sexual discussion before the deed can arouse your partner and help ignite the fire; a sexy talk after the act can be pleasant and serve as a "reminder of what just happened and can help build anticipation for the next encounter." One further reason dirty language is so enjoyable for us is that it helps us feel grounded and causes us to live in the present now. This is something that many of us struggle to accomplish, particularly when we're nude and self-conscious about our breasts or tummies, but nasty chat may help us overcome this challenge. "Many people are not very present during sex," "They may close their eyes, remain silent, or be distracted by thoughts," and "Sex can be a very uncomfortable experience for some people." When you have to be there and interested in the conversation, it makes for a more satisfying sexual experience. If your partner says something like, "I enjoy massaging your thighs," you will subconsciously be aware of their hand being on your body as they perform the action. At long last, it is appropriate to use vulgar language in its most literal sense. "Just the act of talking may be exciting on its own since you are able to feel your lips, tongue, and even your breath when you do so. It's a once in a lifetime opportunity!"

THAT IS THE TYPE OF GIRL YOU SHOULD STRIVE TO GET.

In today's world, if you're lucky enough to find a girl who doesn't like to party for no reason, who doesn't smoke anything, who doesn't do drugs, who doesn't need all of the attention, who doesn't require the materialistic things, who doesn't entertain every cute guy she comes across, who is secure about herself, who doesn't play games with your feelings, who knows how to be loyal to just one man, who is attempting to get her life together, who

You definitely want to spend as much time as possible with her before she enters her teen years. You definitely want to be with her before another guy comes along and hurts her feelings because that's the sort of women you want to be with. You want to be with her before another guy comes along and breaks her, because that's the sort of women you want to be with.

That is the type of lady you want to stay with as long as possible before she gets ruined by a critical mass of others who coerce her into changing. That is the kind of woman with whom you want to develop your relationship and lay the groundwork for its future. That's the type of woman you want to spend years getting to know and passing on your wisdom to, doesn't it? That is the type of woman you one day hope to settle down with, get married to, and have a family with. When you find a girl like that, you should do all in your power to keep her since other females like her are becoming increasingly rare. You definitely do not want to fuck upon the sort of female that you just described. Therefore, you are the luckiest person alive if that girl likes you and she is interested in you. Dote on her. She deserves respect.

Having the Conversation: Why You Should Discuss Sexuality With Your Teenage Child as a Parent.

Teenagers often don't know how to act appropriately when it comes to sexual activity, which is why it's important for parents to provide their children with clear guidelines and assistance so that they can comprehend what it means to become physically attached to another person.

If you truly want your child to take responsibility of her sexuality and not give in to something she is not ready for as a consequence of ignorance, you are the only person who is compelled to do this other than yourself as the parent. No one else is required to do this.

While it can be challenging for parents and might seem somewhat embarrassing for them to communicate their beliefs and expectations to their children, it is important for them to do so.

The majority of parents are afraid of being excluded as a consequence of trying to have this conversation, which is why it is considered a controversial topic to be discussed in the household.

You need to realize that the children we have at home monitor our conduct and that it is via this that they tend to act and behave with their peers, regardless of whether or not they comprehend it is not thought of. This is something that you need to grasp.

These behaviors, in and of themselves, help our child develop their own unique personality. Such as having an understanding of right and wrong.

Take, for instance. If you think it is OK to steal, then your kid will undoubtedly grow up thinking that it is the best thing to do. This might result in her getting in trouble with the law and having to deal with the repercussions of her actions.

The same may be said about their sexuality.

What you begin to exhibit is what kids begin to regard as the standard for behavior.

Because of this, you and your spouse need to start having these discussions with your children as soon after birth as you possibly can.

Many parents are reluctant to play the role of the father or mother figure in their children's lives because they don't want to jeopardize the bond they already have with their children.

You need to have an understanding that teenagers will always have a need for the perspective of their parents in order to aid them through their experience of not becoming lost in making any sexual decision that can have and leave a bad print on them. This includes both narcotics and alcoholic beverages as well.

If you do not do this, the kid will feel abandoned, and as a result, they will be more likely to engage in other social vices, some of which you may not even be aware of given the kind of environment we live in today.

How To Add Humor And Appeal To Your Written Communications

We are going to speak about humor and charm and how these attributes can bring a lot of value to your text messaging experience, especially when engaging with a woman. This is especially important when texting with a woman.

It is important to bear in mind that the successful use of comedy, like the successful application of so many other tactics, involves dexterity and nuance. You should avoid sending someone a text message that contains content that they could find insulting or otherwise unsettling. When in doubt, the safest course of action is almost always to err on the side of caution.

In addition, comedy is contextual and varies according to the recipient of the text message you are sending it. This indicates that you need to keep a watchful eye on the response of the recipient of your message. If they don't laugh or even grin, it's probably better to just chalk it up to a failed attempt and go on to something else.

When you want to use comedy in a text message, the most important thing to keep in mind is that you need to know your receiver. In addition, you should make an effort to strike a healthy balance between contributing to the positive attitude they are presently in and preserving the excellent mood they have already established.

Now that we've established that, let's proceed.

There are many different kinds of jokes, remarks, photos, and memes that might be humorous. Some are light-hearted, while others are caustic. However, there are several situations in which the use of humor has the potential to transform an uninteresting text message discussion into one that possesses a great deal of character, personality, and flare.

The question now is, how can you make comedy work for you? Keep in mind that the interaction you have by text message is the initial point of contact, and because of this, you need to get off to a good start.

It is important to keep in mind that the use of humor and charm should be restrained to appropriate levels. Even if it's beneficial to do both, you shouldn't make it a habit of doing too much of either one. Because of this, she will completely lose whatever interest she may have had in you in the beginning. You are free to overreach, but it is best to avoid alienating individuals if at all possible.

Because everyone's sense of humor is unique to them, it's possible that one lady will think everything you send to be hilarious, while another won't find it amusing at all. Because of this, it is critical to ensure that there is a healthy equilibrium at all times.

Let's take a look at a few different ways you might utilize comedy and charm in the discussion you're having through text.

Using humor and wit.

Everyone enjoys a good laugh, so why not give your best go at telling some jokes? Why not tell her about something you find humorous if you believe she'll find it entertaining? Even though you don't want to come out as disrespectful or offensive, telling her a few lighthearted jokes here and there is a great way to break the ice and let her get to know you better.

Paying her compliments

This is a deft demonstration of the fact that you are an upstanding citizen. Tell her what you found hilarious about her or what she said if you thought anything she did or what she said made you laugh. Complimenting someone with a praise is a wonderful way to show appreciation for their efforts, but be sure you don't go overboard by repeating the same thing many times.

First and foremost, keep in mind that she will be able to discern whether or not the compliments you give her are real and true on your part. If she doesn't find it funny or even likes it, there is certainly something wrong with the way you go about communicating with her via text messages in general. It's be that the moment has come to try something different instead. There is no point in getting worked up if she does not answer favorably to your texts because it is unlikely that she will.

Give her something to be happy about.

Give a girl a cause to grin whenever you text her, regardless of whether it is the first time you are texting her or whether you have been texting her for a very long time. When it comes down to it, this is exactly why you should sprinkle your SMS messages with wit and charisma. Your communication through text message will continue to thrive so long as she has a positive attitude and appears to be having fun with it.

If she doesn't feel comfortable enough with you to laugh at anything or tell her about something humorous, it's probably time to take a step back in your relationship with her.

To summarize, having a sense of humor is an excellent method to win someone's favor as soon as they become acquainted with you. It helps individuals feel at ease and confident, and it improves the experience of sending and receiving text messages.

If you are not certain about carrying it out, then it is probably best not to attempt it at all. Keep in mind that using humor and charm in the way that I have shown above is just one of many possible methods to accomplish so; there are many more ways. There are hundreds more, and you ought to choose with the one that caters the most to your requirements.

The Question Concerning Birds And Bees

Have you ever wondered whether or not your child is old enough to engage in conversations about things like birds and bees?

If this is something you've ever pondered, you're not the only one who has.

I am positive that I have! After all, I am supposed to be the knowledgeable one!

There have been a lot of parents who have been curious about whether or not their kid is old enough to have a conversation about birds and bees.

Continue reading to determine whether or not your child is at an appropriate age for sexuality instruction.

Concerns and doubts that are frequently voiced regarding the children's ages and whether or not they are of a suitable age.

Every parent worries about whether or not their kid is mature enough to learn about things like birds and bees.

Have they reached the age of majority? Will they be able to understand what it is that you are trying to convey? What results can you expect if you give them an excessive amount of information?

Similar questions cross our minds all the time. This applies to myself as well.

To tell you the truth, I've been having some major second thoughts about having a conversation about pornography with my son, who is 10 years old. He is a typical example of one of those extremely inquisitive children who turns to Google to find the solutions to their problems. Consequently, I was anxious that the chats we were having might arouse curiosity in going to see what it was that I was talking about. Thankfully, I was able to catch myself in the act, and a little inspection answered any doubts or alleviated any concerns I had.

The following are some issues that you may have regarding your child's age and whether or not they are old enough (or not).

My child is not old enough to participate in sexuality classes right now.

Both in and out of yes.

Education on sexuality covers a wide range of topics in addition to sexuality itself.

A wide range of additional subjects are brought up for discussion as well, such as bodies, relationships, feelings, diversity, consent, attitudes and values, safety, and self-care.

Even if your kid is too young to understand the concept of sexuality, you may start having conversations with them about other issues, such as their feelings or their bodies.

My youngster will not understand a word that I say.

They were capable of understanding, but they were also incapable of doing so.

If they are unable to grasp what you have said, they will just forget it since, from their perspective, it does not make any sense. In addition to this, they could ask for more information.

Give your child a response to one of their many questions that is extremely difficult, even though you are aware that they will not grasp it. Instead of discussing how cows generate milk, you may explain the many steps that are involved in bringing milk from the farm to your table.

For instance, a cow eats some grass, which causes her udders to create milk; the farmer milks the cow; a truck collects the milk; the milk is then transported to a facility for bottling, where it is homogenized and pasteurized... Are you starting to yawn because you're bored yet?

Your child is likely to grow disinterested and stop listening if you respond to their question with such a lengthy and detailed explanation (particularly if you include any industry-specific lingo in your response).

Make sure you follow up with them the next day to find out what they were able to recall from the previous day. I have no doubt that they will not remember very much (if anything at all).

It will consist of an enormous quantity of data.

Possibly, but it's important to bear in mind that toddlers frequently forget what they can't understand.

And studies have shown that having sexual conversations with youngsters does not make them more likely to participate in sexual behavior themselves.

This article may provide you with further information on the advantages of sexuality education as well as the ways in which it may assist our children in making more informed sexual decisions.

I believe that I will hold off till they are a little bit older.

You could, but it's possible that you'll never find the right time to start talking about birds and bees.

Keep in mind that sexuality education covers a lot more ground than just sexuality. It's important to sit down and have a chat with your kid about everything that will assist them in making intelligent decisions regarding love, sex, and relationships.

It is very inappropriate to bring up sexual topics with my kid.

There is no one set of guidelines to follow when it comes to having sexual conversations with youngsters.

It is dependent on a number of factors, such as the age difference between your children and the other children in the neighborhood, whether or not your children go to school, whether or not they listen to music on the radio or watch television, and the type of community in which you live....

My home is located in the middle of the city, which is where the majority of the 'sex stores,' brothels, and sex workers are. My children were exposed to topics like sex toys and prostitution much before they would have normally shown interest in topics of this nature. However, as a result of people seeing it, they ask questions regarding it. My challenge as a parent is to provide them with information that is suitable for their age on a subject that is not suitable for their age.

Managing challenging issues and questions

If you're lucky, your youngster will start inquiring after things at some point. When kids get interested in something, like the topic of "where do babies come from?", they commonly ask questions about it.

If someone asks a question about a topic, it indicates that they are interested in gaining further knowledge about that topic. It should come as no surprise that now is the appropriate time to initiate sexuality conversations with young people. It might be something that comes naturally to their interest, such as wanting to know where babies come from. Oral sex or pornography are two examples of topics that might be confusing to someone who isn't naturally interested in them but has been brought to their attention by someone else.

Research as well as anecdotal information can teach us about the development of sexuality in children in a healthy way. In addition, when a child grows older, their sexual development continues to improve, and they begin to display certain sexual behaviors, they also begin to get intrigued by certain topics, including where babies come from.

The fact that you are blessed with a youngster that is curious in the world around them is a wonderful thing. Because all you have to do is react to their questions and engage in conversation about the things that are important to them. Because your child has already started talking about it, you don't need to worry about forgetting to bring up the subject of where babies come from!

In addition to this, you have full control over the content that kids consume, so you can make sure that it is suitable for their age group. They consider you to be an honest and reliable source of information! This is really necessary if you want to maintain control over the material that your children are exposed to.

It also suggests that your child understands that you are open to talking about anything; the majority of children understand that if they can talk to you about sex, then they can talk to you about anything!

The following are some examples of different types of confidence:

Money: People who have an excessive amount of money or authority typically have a high level of self-confidence since they are aware that money can fix just about any problem. Some women go out of their way to find wealthy men, and the fact that finding one is difficult leads them to overlook any inappropriate behavior on the part of the men they date.

Sports and exercise both raise levels of the hormone testosterone and the feel-good chemical endorphin in the body. When you put in a lot of effort, overcome obstacles, and finally see the fruit of your labor, it inherently gives you a sense of value and significance since you are aware that not everyone can do what you have.

Family and close friends – When you are surrounded by people who love you for who you are, it is much easier to appreciate the positive connections you have and to have a lower emotional reaction to those who do not appear to like you for no apparent reason.

Your ego and reputation will receive a boost among your contemporaries as well as among other ladies if you have a girlfriend who you feel attractive and that also loves you.

Being in a position of authority, particularly one in which other people depend on you, may be beneficial to one's feeling of self-assurance.

Having an additional source of money in addition to your normal employment may be a source of confidence. This is especially true if you are the one who is responsible for developing this additional source of revenue. This ties into the idea of personal choices and preferences. If you just have one source of income, you are entirely reliant on your employer. However, having numerous sources of money decreases the other person's equity in your life, which in turn provides you with sufficient self-assurance to engage in risky behavior without fear of repercussions.

Talent - Having talent in an endeavor that other people value automatically raises the worth of the person possessing that talent. This gives you a sense of superiority and makes you less replaceable in the long run.

What is Effective in Sexual Education and What Is Not?

It is not a secret that sexuality education is a contentious issue in today's society. Just consider all of the arguments that have been made on the subject matter that should be taught in schools.

Others believe that sexuality education should be more thorough, including instruction on abstinence as well as other methods of birth control, while others are of the opinion that it should simply cover the topic of abstinence.

When it comes to sex education, there is no simple solution to be found. But there is one fact that cannot be argued: the significance of the role that parents play in the sexuality education of their offspring cannot be overstated.

It is essential to have an open and honest discussion about sexuality with your adolescent child, regardless of the opinions you hold about sexuality yourself.

When having a conversation about sexuality with your adolescent, it's important to keep the following in mind:

- Maintain candor and openness: It is essential to discuss sexuality in an open and honest manner with your adolescent. This requires that you be willing to answer any questions that they may have, despite the fact that it may feel awkward to do so.

- Exercise proper courtesy: It is essential that you show respect for your teenager's thoughts, feelings, and beliefs at all times. Keep in mind that you are not attempting to persuade them of anything; rather, your goal is to simply present facts and answer any questions they may have.

- Don't overcomplicate things: When it comes to sexuality instruction, less words are better. Make an effort to center yourself on fundamental topics such as human anatomy, reproduction, and sexually transmitted diseases (STDs). It is not necessary to go into the specifics, even the most minute ones, unless your adolescent specifically requests for them.

- Always be ready: It is completely fine if you do not feel comfortable discussing sexuality. Just make sure that you do some study in advance so that you are prepared to answer any questions that your teenager may have.

Teaching Your Child About the Various Expressions of Affection Made by Other People

The process of sexuality education is not always easy. There are many ways that individuals may express their love for one another, and not all of them include sexual contact.

It is crucial to educate your adolescent about the many methods in which individuals display affection for one another so that they may better comprehend not just their own feelings but also the feelings of others.

The following are some of the various ways individuals express their love for one another:

Hugging, kissing, and holding hands are all examples of forms of physical contact that fall under this category.

Everything That Your Youngster Needs to Know Concerning Consent

When it comes to teaching consent in sex education for children aged 8 to 12 years old, it is essential to emphasize on the concept of consent rather than on the specifics of sex.

This requires having conversations about respecting the limits and feelings of other people and having a knowledge that everyone has the freedom to say yes or no to having physical contact with another person.

It is also essential to have an open conversation about consent with your kid and to ensure that they comprehend the necessity of consent at all times, including when it comes to interactions between individuals who are already familiar with one another.

Teach your kid that permission is something that may be modified or withdrawn at any moment, and that this change or withdrawal must be honored by everyone involved.

You may use common examples, such as cooking a snack together, playing a game, or using the family computer, to assist explain the concept of consent in a manner that is acceptable for the child's age.

Ensure that your kid understands that consent must be gained before to participating in any activity, and that it may be revoked at any moment, even if it was previously granted.

Let's pretend that your kid is interested in playing a game of tag with a buddy of theirs. It is necessary for them to exchange consent before they begin playing the game.

Even if it is simply a game, they have the responsibility of making sure their friend is familiar with the guidelines and is interested in participating.

You may inquire of them, "Are you comfortable with playing tag?

Do you mind if I try to catch up with you? Are there any guidelines that we ought to abide by?"

Before participating in any physical activities, this will help your child better comprehend the concept of permission.

Stories provide yet another illustration of the concept of permission. Your youngsters will enjoy hearing a story about two friends who go to the park together and play.

For instance, Friend A is interested in jumping on the trampoline, while Friend B does not wish to participate in this activity. In this scenario, Friend A is obligated to take into consideration the preferences of Friend B and come up with an alternate activity that they may enjoy together.

This demonstrates how crucial it is for all of the individuals involved to communicate their thoughts and feelings to one another and to respect the decisions that each other makes.

2. Words of affirmation, such as "I love you," "I'm proud of you," or just expressing thanks. This can include things like stating "I love you" or "I'm proud of you."

3. Spending quality time together means engaging in activities with another person that need your full attention, such as having a conversation, going on a date, or simply spending time together.

4. Performing acts of service for another person, such as preparing meals, cleaning, or running errands on their behalf.

5. Gifts are a considerate approach to show someone that you care about them

by giving them something that shows you've put some thinking into it.

It is essential to keep in mind that different people communicate their feelings of affection in different ways. It's possible that some individuals favor one form of attachment over another. Remember that just because someone does not show their passion for you in a physical form, it does not imply that they do not care about you. This is a very essential point to keep in mind.

It is always advisable to ask someone directly how they are feeling if you are unsure of how they are currently feeling. It's important to have this talk in order to clear up any misunderstandings, but it may be nerve-wracking to do so.

Guidelines For Unclean Conversations

To be able to turn a woman on or spice things up in a room, one of the skills that all guys should master is talking filthy. It's an excellent way to spice things up. In any event, it is tough, and there is no tried-and-true method to accomplish it because every relationship is unique and every women like different things. Nevertheless, it is possible to do it. There is not much of a distinction between nauseating talk and nasty conversation, and the two are nearly on par with one another. In order to provide you with aid in finding the appropriate things to say, we spoke with a small group of Dirty speaking women regarding sexual discussion. Through these conversations, we discovered that there are a few guidelines that the majority of women can agree with.

Make an effort to avoid using words that show contempt. It is really inconvenient for me to have a reputation as a prostitute. Please don't make any references to my breasts or cleavage.

as the nickname "cunt." These kinds of words are causing a ruckus. The fact that you don't intend for it to be an insult doesn't change the reality that we hear words

like things and naturally experience a negative surge as a result of the fact that those words are frequently used in conversation.

On the other hand. It pulls us out of existence and sets us completely separate from anything else. Aggregate buzz killer, and sometimes (but not always)

an adversary.

Please let me know that you find me appealing. I absolutely like it when a man just lifts my body off the bed when we're having sex.

down and makes it clear that I'm being provocative. It bolsters my confidence, gives me a tingling feeling all over, and immediately

causes me to feel the urge to take some action to bring about the same reaction in him.

Please don't give me any instructions about how to stay calm. During the time when I was having sexual relations with a former partner who was having problems,

reaching its zenith, and I enquired, "Are you all right?" ...and he spoke the word "Shhh" so that he could concentrate. It was just incredible.

rude, and he gave off the impression that he was having sexual intercourse with a blow-up doll. In summary, he was just as offensive as the blow-up doll.

gratified in every way. Unquestionably, he did not bring everything to a close.

Please keep me informed that you need to complete this task all through the night. No matter what we are doing, there is nothing that can create a young girl.

listening to whatever her man is listening to makes her feel superior to everything else, thus she wants him to keep doing it. It indicates that he has attained his goals, and thus

As long as I find that I enjoy it too, it will motivate me to move through with my plans.

It is best not to suggest that someone not use a condom. If we don't go through with it, it won't matter how exciting you try to make it sound.

since we don't know one another that well, I won't have any urge to 'rawdog this' with you. In the first place, due to the fact that I don't

know you all around okay, and two, since that sounds revolting to me despite the fact that you seem to be doing OK.

The command is to. A significant portion of our life as women reveals the reality about how much control we have over our surroundings and how much care we take.

to the point that having somebody else take charge and be responsible for us is a welcome relief from the pressure caused by other people. Now consider this:

I give you permission to tell me what you want me to do or what you need me to do. A man who is both numerous and talkative is attractive, and

It eliminates a fraction of the labor that I would have to undertake in order to do anything else.

Make an effort not to be condescending. Having said that, somebody once pointed out to me that I was doing a certain action in the wrong way.

Adding insult to injury, I perished right away. I was left with the impression that I was a total failure, and I do not wish to.

continue having sexual intercourse with the person who was responsible for making me feel that way. If there's anything you'd like me to do, please let me know.

things in an unanticipated manner, simply propose something different, and don't let me know that I'm handling it poorly or severely.

Please call me by my name. It indicates that he is available and interested in the event, and it gives me the impression that he is interested in what I have to say.

I am a completely different young person. It is uncomfortable, especially when he whispers my name in my ear as he is touching me.

Please let me know how good it is to be here. The connection between people and the times and places in which they engage in sexual activity always reveals the unvarnished reality.

There is a market for names. It bolsters the idea that we are sharing this moment in time together very well.

It is best to avoid becoming too specialized. When referring to the specialist's office, the words "penis" and "vagina" were only suggested.

the room itself. In terms of buzz and execution, that is a certain buzz execute. If I needed to make myself comfortable

I would make an appointment with my gynecologist after seeing my specialist.

 Please let me know how wonderful I feel and how my food tastes.Complimentsare very appreciated by young women, but if you merely remark "you look beautiful," they may become uncomfortable.

If we keep telling you, "You are so hot/attractive/lovely," the compliment will eventually lose its meaning, and all we will do is say it.

Consider that you have nothing further to add to the conversation. In the event that you believe that I smell, taste, or feel wonderful, please let me know. It can appear that way, yet

Although it seems strange to you, we welcome the opportunity to hear it.

Men's Psychology: A Look Inside The Minds Of Men

Is It Something That They Were Born With?

It's been believed that males are much more rational than women throughout the years, but does this stereotype hold water? Should this truly be utilized as a factor in determining who has the greater amount of life experience, despite the fact that the biblical account of evolution describes how the woman came into existence as a result of the male having lived first?

Men, for instance, have been known to and shown to think in an archaic manner, in which they attribute having several sexual partners to their nature. However, where is the logic in that? If you ask me, the reason why there is such a thing as a woman is because, without the woman's touch, man would have failed horribly in all of his endeavors.

So, we already know that men need us in order to find consolation in this world, and we also know that we are an essential component in that recipe; yet, we don't just walk in, do we? If we do it, we make sure to do it in a way that leaves a lasting impact. The days are long gone when there was plenty of time to squander trying things out ineffectively before ultimately succeeding at them. Due to the fact that life is too short, along with the fact that work schedules are demanding and the economy is demanding, it does not make sense to continue wasting precious time going wrong with love.

You've undoubtedly messed up countless other relationships in the past, but for some reason, you feel that this one is worth going all the way with. You like this guy. You are not an expert due to the fact that you have been testing for the longest time now, and it is true that you may still end up losing this one if you are not equipped appropriately. Therefore, it is clear that there is a requirement to comprehend the thoughts that go through the heads of individuals, and this is an excellent beginning.

The Way That They Think

If you believe that having sexual relations is the most important thing for them, you are gravely mistaken. It is true that there will be occasions when they go out baiting to catch simply because of a bet, and there will also be instances when they'll go seeking simply because the home became dull; nevertheless, in the back of their thoughts, these are only pathetic excuses to discover the one that is worth abandoning the "game play." In spite of the fact that you fit that description perfectly, what exactly is it that you are supposed to be doing here? Here are three of the most compelling underlying realities about how guys perceive things and reason out in the world that you were previously unaware of.

Men Can Become Insecure

It's possible that this one took you by surprise, but dang it, that's the truth. You have to understand that women have a propensity to talk about everything, including their sentiments, their problems with boys, their families, their friends, and in general anything that revolves around them. However, communicating one's thoughts and working things out via conversation is frequently a man's last recourse. Instead, you should ask him to brag about his latest catch. It won't take long for him to start talking about it.

If you are a woman and you hear that other women are considered as gossipers and you feel insulted by this, it is likely because you are more knowledgeable about this topic than other women. The ability to juggle many responsibilities at once is one of the many strengths of having a female partner. She is merely a sociable human who enjoys chatting while she works; if males want to perceive this all in a bad light, we still know better. She likes to converse while she is doing her tasks.

Women have a far easier time articulating their emotions than males do, which is one of the reasons why even the most self-assured men still harbora "insecure little boy" inside of them. Men, like women, have fears and anxieties; they have issues about their looks and their feelings; conversing with another person about these things would be quite freeing for them.

Do you find yourself wondering why he won't just let everything go off the rails? Because throughout the course of history, men have learned that any indication of weakness on their part puts them open to mockery, he won't because of this realization. If he were to open up, it would have to be to a male counterpart, and let's face it, he would be the joke of the day, and possibly be considered as less of a man if he did that.

Restoring The Appeal Of The Attraction

Honey, how many times have you heard yourself say, "Not today. If you want to avoid getting intimate or having sex with your spouse, why not use the excuse, "I have a headache," or a similar comment, as a sneaky way to get out of it? Honey, I'm sorry but not tonight! I'll assume that as a busy woman, you're familiar with the feeling of not being in the mood, being pressured for time, or just not having the energy to do something. What does it mean, though, when the statement "Not tonight, honey" becomes your signature catchphrase?

It is so easy to let a romantic relationship fizzle out and develop the terrible habit of overworking yourself to the point of exhaustion, falling asleep in front of the television, stumbling into bed, and sleeping with your partner's back. Before you know it, a month has gone by, and you're fighting about little matters that weren't previously a source of contention between the two of you. Whether your time and energy are being sucked by children or you are concentrating on expanding your business, by the end of the evening, sex is often the last thing on your mind.

I'll be honest with you and say that, as a woman who has a history of sexual abuse that extends back many years, I wasn't always all that enthused about sex throughout my 20-year marriage, especially when my weight was on my mind. I have a history of sexual abuse that stretches back many years. I'll be honest with you and say that. The fact that I constantly reminded myself that I was overweight and unattractive prevented me from establishing healthy boundaries with my body and caused me to feel like a victim. This brought back memories of when I was a little child with no concept of boundaries and a deep-seated fear of grownup males.

For me to be able to deal with my many trust issues and avoid the tendency to let my paranoia of men in general affect my relationship with my husband, I've had to use a technique known as the Emotional Freedom Technique (EFT) to handle the many stresses that come up in my life related to being a woman and feeling safe around sex. I've had to do this in order to use the EFT to handle the many stresses that come up in my life related to being a woman.

This makes me think about programming again.

Amy, a lovely young woman from Bedford, Indiana, who would later become extremely significant to me, had been visiting a psychologist who I was familiar with back in the day. She had been brought up in a traditional Christian home in a nice family, which is to say a family that consisted of kind and honorable people, and she was married to a guy whom she cherished as well as looked up to. She was the secretary in the emergency room at the hospital in the next town, and she was a mother to two great children. She also had a job that she adored working in the hospital. According to her standards, she had accomplished her goals and was content with her life.

However, by the time she was 28, she had begun to actively seek out sexual experiences that were both anonymous and demeaning with guys who were frequently aggressive. In fewer than three years, she suffered the loss of both her husband and her children while also being separated from her religion.

She sought assistance and realized, if somewhat belatedly, that when she witnessed people at the hospital who she believed were more deserving of happiness than herself experiencing unhappiness, she would feel as though she was not deserving of the benefits that she had been given. Her inherent sensitivity, along with the conviction that she was unworthy, had a role in the development of circumstances that led to the loss of those blessings.

Sexuality And Having Children

If someone knows the magic answer to how to mix a satisfying sex life with becoming a parent, then please let me know so that I may pass it on to the appropriate people. After a frantic day of continually satisfying the requests of the prince and princesses and of being clambered on, climbed over, and caressed all day long, the last thing I want at night is more physical contact. At this point in time, I have three children who are younger than six years old, and I am writing this while taking care of them. I have this hankering to be alone in my bed, like a lonely starfish that is drifting aimlessly in the ocean. The fact that my children are still so little probably means that I'm going through the toughest part of it right now, although I've heard that the teenage years aren't much better.

In this chapter, we will discuss the various ways in which you and your partner may continue to have a satisfying sexual life despite the fact that you both now have children. Exhaustion, hormones, the recovery period after giving birth, the dread of becoming pregnant, pain experienced during sex, feelings of self-consciousness, and hectic schedules are all factors that can have a detrimental impact on our sexual life. Even when faced with challenges, married spouses have a duty to make every effort to be physically committed to one another and to remain together. The saying of the Apostle Paul is:

Do not deny one another anything unless you both agree to do so for a certain period of time so that you can devote yourself to prayer and fasting, and then gather back together after that so that Satan will not be able to entice you due to your lack of self-control.

How to Conquer Your Social Anxiety and Shyness

The majority of the time, conversation comes easily. Since we were children and first learned how to form words and comprehend what they meant, the two of us have been engaged in conversation. Talking is simple, but what about trash talking? That's a completely different ballgame entirely. When it comes to engaging in lighthearted, amusing pillow conversation, even the most talkative, chatty, outgoing, and sociable personalities face a speed block. Even the statements you have read up to this point may have made you shift uncomfortably in your seat or flush from head to toe at the mere prospect of repeating these sentences out to your spouse. If this is the case, you are not alone. It's difficult to get some words and phrases out of your mouth, let alone out of your head. Even the most sexually self-assured individual is guaranteed to have at least one or two filthy words in their vocabulary that may cause them to flush bright red with humiliation. Why do we respond in such a manner? On other occasions, we have no issue expressing our viewpoints, even if no one else is interested in listening to them. Dirty chat, on the other hand, might make you feel tongue-tied, agitated, and nervous all at once. This is because engaging in sexual activity has traditionally been more about "doing" than it has been about "talking."

When you start talking trash in front of a potential new partner, it's the same as taking your clothes off. You are anxious and can't help but wonder what they are thinking and how they are feeling. Every time you say a new word or phrase, it feels as like another article of your clothes is being removed, and the whole time, you're wondering if they like it or not. Is it something that turns them on? Or, to make matters worse, is it turning them away? When you do this, do people think it's a sexual gesture? Do they want you to quit what you're doing? Because there are so many things to consider, it is not surprising that developing our carnal confidence vocally is not the simplest process. If you and your partner have never done anything like this in front of each other before, the unexpected use of obscene language may take both of you off guard or even startle you.

The First Step Toward Overcoming Your Reserve is to Practicing with Yourself

It is going to be challenging for a lot of people to get over their shyness, so before you start trying out some of your newly discovered dirty vocabulary out on your partner, it is a better idea to practice on yourself first so you can get the feel of it and become comfortable with the concept of speaking this out loud. You should begin by selecting a few phrases or sentences, and then you should try talking nasty to yourself while you are masturbating. You don't need to worry about sounding ridiculous because no one can actually hear you anyhow. Talking nasty to yourself while masturbating is a great way to increase your level of pleasure. Put your attention on the joy you are experiencing and say what you think and how you really feel. The use of straightforward expressions such as "Oh yes, that feels so damn good" is already a step in the right direction. It's better than being quiet, and the more you practice continually talking to yourself, the less weird it is with each practice session you do. It's better than keeping quiet, anyhow.

Here Are Four Ways That You Can Make Indecent Talk More Enjoyable.

It may be unnerving when someone refers to your body using a language that doesn't seem quite right to you. Have a talk with your significant other about the types of conversations that you two could find entertaining.

In response to this, you should inquire about any irritants or ways of speaking that they have a strong preference towards. If you are going to engage in any kind of insulting language or linguistic power play, make sure that both parties are having fun with the dialogue, and do it with care.

Strengthen your self-assurance.

When you do anything for the first time, it may take all of your guts to even utter a single word. However, as time goes on, you'll find that it gets simpler and more straightforward. If you find that talking while sensually aroused makes you uncomfortable, try masturbating alone and having a conversation with yourself while you're doing it. This is especially helpful if you're feeling shy.

Additionally, if there is an item of clothing you can wear or another action you can do to radiate confidence, it will be much simpler for you to engage in a hostile conversation.

Remember that this is not only a sex-related instrument in any way, shape, or form. In point of fact, it may be difficult for many people to concentrate on discussion when they are in the midst of enjoying themselves. As an alternative, you might use insulting words as a form of foreplay in order to increase your partner's enthusiasm in having sex with you.

Get your spouse excited about what's to come, or better yet, get yourself excited about it!

Consider having a conversation about things that the two of you like doing. After you've had sexual activity, you should talk about the most exciting parts and maybe even the parts you didn't enjoy. After that, the next time the two of you are reunited, you will be more experienced lovers!

Be trustworthy.

What you hear instead are words that are uncomfortable but sincere, which is far superior than duplicating sentences that sound manufactured. Because we are able to tell whether the people we are in relationships with are being serious, cultivating meaningful connections with our partners may be accomplished by studying subjects that are of genuine interest to both parties.

Instead of allowing performance to take precedence over enjoyment, be in touch with your body and pay attention to the sorts of nasty thoughts that come into your head. Best of luck on your adventures!

, there is nowhere else I'd rather be than within or on top of you. Isn't that better now?

Demand Effort From Her In Exchange For The Information.

In the same vein, you should try to avoid providing answers immediately after she has asked for them. This brings back too strong of memories of when I was being interviewed for jobs.

Her: So, what exactly do you do for a living?

You: "I make my living at McDonald's."

Her: Do you really think that?

You: Yes, I'm in charge of the fryers here.

Her: Huh, I was not anticipating that at all.

You: I wouldn't say that at all. That is only a test to see whether or not you are trying to get anything for nothing.

She is currently more curious in the things that you really do. But don't stop fooling about.

Her: So, tell me, what is it that you actually do?

You: "I'm the one who drives the septic truck."

Her: Oh, I'm sorry to hear that.

You are a schmuck. However, I am able to keep it together.

Continue doing it right up until the point where it stops being humorous. Because she will have to exert effort to acquire this knowledge, she perceives you to be more intriguing. The effort that she puts in to find the solution is an investment on her part. She has already put money into it, and as a result, she wants to convince herself that it was a wise decision. Therefore, she is more likely to remain around since she thinks that you are a highly intriguing guy for her to learn more about in the future.

Take this action rather than revealing the secret and immediately handing up the farm. This gives you the opportunity to gauge her interest in you as well.

Play down the magnificence that you possess.

Have you ever noticed how the general public adores white billionaire Warren Buffet yet despises white billionaire Donald Trump to an extreme degree?

One of them brags about their accomplishments more than the other, despite the fact that they are both wealthy and accomplished. When you reach a certain level of accomplishment, the ability to downplay that achievement is a significant contributor to your likeability.

It is best to keep one's success under wraps, even if it was well-deserved and painstakingly gained. Why do lottery winners end up broke so quickly? just because they want to flaunt their wealth and be associated with it. They have not been taught the correct way to apply it in their work. However, Warren Buffet tends to play down his lavish lifestyle. Even if he has the ability to do so, he does not fritter away money on unnecessary indulgences, frivolous purchases, or a costly way of life.

The most important thing to learn from this is to take it easy. Do not exaggerate the significance of your previous successes and all that is wonderful about you. Also, try to avoid being easily excited. Or you are so anxious to show off your accomplishments.

Women are able to look straight through this. When it comes to issues of this nature, they have a good idea of the sort of man you are and will divide you into one of three categories: A person who is worthless in whatever way. B. A person who has recently discovered something of worth and can't stop talking about it. C. On the other hand, there are gentlemen who take life easy, revel in their achievements, but don't make a big deal out of it.

There's a sweet spot of modesty that works perfectly for this situation. If she compliments you by saying, "Wow, you're really good at..." just respond, "Not really, I've just been doing it long enough."

She will be aware that is not the case. And the understatement is the one that she will enjoy the most out of all the possible responses.

School Learning

This involves delivering comprehensive sexuality education that is present in the classroom instruction, school policy and practice, as well as in the partnerships that the school establishes with the local community and with you. There is a provision in the law that enables parents to provide their children an appropriate and comprehensive sexuality education.

Avoiding capturing private moments on camera is a valuable lesson that should be incorporated into the curriculum.

The government ought to make sure that sex education include gender equality as well.

It is required to specify which methods of birth control are appropriate for teenagers. For instance, among all other methods of birth control, the condom is always an excellent choice as a birth control technique since it does not have any hormonal side effects, it is simple to purchase, and it is convenient to use.

Masturbation should be mentioned as a further consideration as well. It refers to the act of touching one's genitalia in any way. Masturbation is associated with a wide variety of positive and negative outcomes. However, doing so in a reasonable amount is perfectly OK, however doing so in an excessive amount will always be hazardous to the body.

You may retain your sanity by masturbating since it releases tension in your body. Improves the quality of sleep.

When used in excessive amounts, it is also associated with a number of adverse consequences. When done to an excessive degree, it will have an effect on both your body and your mind.

Methods for Providing Sexual Education to Young People

It may be a very awkward conversation to have with youngsters of school age regarding sexual topics. However, there are some topics that ought to be talked freely with children in order to dispel any uncertainties that they may have.

It's never too early to start a conversation with your kid about real-life topics like puberty and pregnancy. For instance, if a member of the family is expecting a child, you should explain to her how a child grows inside of a woman's body.

You might even let your youngster to watch a television show on love and relationships for a short period of time.

Parents have a responsibility to talk to their preteen and teenage children about the dangers of the internet, including sexting and sexual abuse. You have a responsibility to be aware of the repercussions of sharing naked images.

It is important that young people have enough understanding about the impacts of substances like alcohol and drugs.

Why is education on sexual health so vital for the overall health and well-being of young people? At each and every grade level, students get instruction that is both comprehensive and sexual health-focused. You can aid young people by providing them with the following, in addition to support from their parents and the community: Avoid having unfavorable effects on your health. Every year in the United States, there are around 750,000 adolescent females who become pregnant, and up to 82 percent of those pregnancies are unplanned. Teenagers between the ages of 15 and 24 are responsible for a quarter of all new HIV infections in the United States. Furthermore, adolescents are responsible for about half of the more than 19 million new STD infections that occur annually in the United States. Young people are equipped with the knowledge and skills necessary to defend themselves thanks to sexual education.

Find Out If She Is Interested In You And How To Tell

There are several telltale signals that might assist you in determining whether the lady you are messaging is interested in you. If you are unsure about this, you should look for these signs. In the next section, we will instruct you on how to determine whether or not she has an interest in you. There are also a few things you can say to her in a text message that will pique her interest in you, which is useful if you want to take the discussion to the next level.

If she responds to you within a few minutes, you may assume that she is interested in what you have to say. It's possible that she was really busy and only now saw your message; on the other hand, it's also possible that she truly wants to chat to you.

If you have the impression that she is flirting with you as well, it is a strong indicator that she has an interest in you. This in no way indicates that she is prepared for a date or a sexual connection of any kind. To the point when she thinks she's ready to take things to the next level, a little flirting now and again might sometimes move her closer to that place. If you and your companion have moved on from one subject to another in the course of your discussion, you could be heading in the direction of something more significant. If you start chatting to her about more personal subjects, you run the risk of having this happen.

If she is attempting to get more personal with you by asking questions about your life or making predictions about what you would do in a given circumstance, then this is typically an indication that she's interested in you. For example, if she asks you what you would do in a certain situation or asks you about your life, then she may be interested in you. We humans are naturally quite inquisitive. If we did not find the other person interesting, we would not go to the trouble of asking them so many questions.

If she brings up her future plans while she's chatting to you, there's a strong likelihood that she wants to include you in those plans. Perhaps she is planning a trip or is considering a career change at this time. These things frequently result in the beginning of new adventures and connections with other individuals. If it appears as though all she wants to know about is the specifics of your life and she is at ease sharing her own with you, then it is possible that you will be embarking on an exciting journey with her.

It's possible that she's starting to plan out when she'll next get to see you. This is one of the most significant indicators that she could be interested in you as a potential partner. If you spend time together, she will want to get together with you again in the future. This can be a clue that she likes you or wants to get to know you better.

It's possible that she's relaying all of this information to you because she's aware that if you're interested in her, then there's a strong probability that she should investigate whether or not things are serious between the two of you. If she is attempting to get personal with you, then there is a good chance that the two of you have more in store for one other in the future.

When individuals start getting into the mindset of being in a relationship, the next step for the majority of them is to talk about their goals for the future. This sort of stuff being said by women is not unheard of by any means, but it does happen far less frequently than it does by men. The majority of women are interested in hearing how your relationship is doing. If you give off the impression that you are enthusiastic and interested in her, there is a strong probability that she is beginning to feel the same way about you.

If she is considering how the two of you could spend the rest of your lives together, then this is excellent news for the two of you. It's possible that she likes you and wants to start a relationship with you soon, so take this as a hint that she's interested in you. If there are a lot of these kinds of ideas exchanged through text, then it's more probable that there is something significant about the two of you moving ahead together. This might happen when women start thinking about their hopes and aspirations for their shared future.

If she is starting to discuss some of her ambitions with you, then it is a sign that she is getting closer to the beginning of a relationship with you. It's possible that she has ambitions that she's never discussed with anybody else. It's possible that she's never shared any of this information with anybody else before, and this is one of the first times she's done so. When women are ready for a committed relationship, they will begin communicating things like this with their partners, such as how they feel about the relationship.

It's possible that she feels the same way about you if you know that something is about to happen and you can't wait for it to happen. This might be an indication that she likes you. It's possible that she has something, like a date or a sexual encounter, planned for the two of you to do together in the near future. Sometimes all that women desire from their guys is to have a sexual encounter with them.

Things That Can Get You And Your Partner Talking About Sexuality To Start A Conversation

Our sexual lives are a complete disaster. According to certified clinical psychologist Dr. Mimi Shagaga, it is normal to feel uncomfortable when initially beginning something new. "Sex can be a taboo subject for many people," Dr.Shagaga explained. "If you have concerns about sexuality or body shape, it could be a sensitive issue," he added. "Most of the time it has to do with the fact that sex was discussed in my childhood/family." However, you should not be scared. It is possible to have sexual conversations with your spouse in a way that is as uncomplicated as possible.

The following are some methods in which you may start a meaningful discussion that can assist you in having the most amazing sexual experience of your life:

Pick a time when things are quiet and you can just relax.

Elisa Boquin, a certified psychotherapist and sex therapist at LMFT, emphasizes that it is crucial to pay attention to the setting in which you and your spouse discuss sexual matters. Because we are at our most sensitive state and are prone to being misinterpreted, you shouldn't try to chat to them while or after we've had sex. Talk to them when they are both silent and not amused. "Before we get started, I wanted to take a break and chat to my partner about some ways that I may expand my sexual life. "Do you think this is a good time?" According to Bokin.

What shall we say?

If you are unsure how to begin a discussion, the following are some easy conversation starters that you may use:

"How is our sex life now?"

"How much do you enjoy our sex life?"

"Do you like our sex life?"

"Are you hesitant to talk about aspects of your sexuality out of fear? What was your greatest concern over my possible response, and why?"

"I really like the way you ___ during sex."

"There are several topics that I would want to discuss with you. Would you want to hear about it?

"Would you like to do something else with sex?"

"Have you ever been sexually embarrassed by me?"

"How can we make sure we talk freely about sex?"

It is essential to avoid making your spouse feel as though they are being attacked, and the simplest approach to avoid this is to remind them of the wonderful things they have accomplished. Investigate the aspects of your sexual life that you enjoy and would like to maintain, and then have a conversation about the aspects that you would like to alter.

It is essential to have a dialogue with your spouse about the things you enjoy and hate. Although this can be a challenging discussion, the ideal partner is one who is attentive and open to the dynamics of the relationship.

How do you choose the aspects of something you wish to alter?

It is essential to communicate your desires if you get the impression that your requirements are not being satisfied. First, determine whether or not any of your needs have been addressed, and then focus on them. For instance, a partner may end up achieving an orgasm before the other can, leading the other to believe that the intercourse is at an end. Or perhaps your spouse is reluctant to attempt oral sex, although you can't get enough of it.

There is an infinite number of possibilities, and no topic may be too light or too heavy to discuss with the person with whom one is having sexual relations. It seems to me that it would be best to listen to the input, and if I were to answer "yes," I would then consult a partner. It begins with what it is that you are lacking. What would you say to someone who has a lot of things, doesn't blame their coworkers, and is willing to share whatever they want? Is it permissible to say things to me that are harmful regarding my sexual life? I have recently come to the realization that I love/like ___ more, and it hurts my heart to do this since it is not necessary. Would you be interested in hearing some suggestions that might assist me in meeting these needs?'

It is not necessary for you to completely abandon ship just because your spouse is unable to fulfill all of your expectations; their limits may not coincide with the goals that you have set for the relationship. Sex therapy might be helpful in this situation since it can teach you how to better handle your lack of desire.

www.ingramcontent.com/pod-product-compliance
Lightning Source LLC
Chambersburg PA
CBHW050414120526
44590CB00015B/1960